"Those familiar with K. A. Opperman's pastoral Halloween poetry may be surprised at how deep into the darkness he ventures without a jack-o'-lantern to guide him. But those brave enough to follow will be rewarded with glimpses of sublime beauty such as are only seen by moonlight when the Devil is loosed from chains."—Adam Bolivar, author of *Ballads for the Witching Hour*

"K. A. Opperman's *The Laughter of Ghouls* is a dark gem of endless depths in which one may see the decadent procession of exquisite darkness in which this poet revels!"—D. L. Myers, author of *Oracles from the Black Pool*

"Opperman's first collection of dark poetry, 2015's *The Crimson Tome*, was a promising debut. This new collection represents a maturing, both of technical skill and the depth and emotionality of his work. . . . Be prepared, thus, for crumbling stone work and mist-ensnared forests, exquisite beauties and suggestive fungus, graves both premature and reopened, for roses, nightmares and blood. . . . This collection establishes Opperman as one of a select band of contemporary poets who do not fear to draw from the past in order to illuminate the present with a Beltane fire. But you will read this book for the sheer pleasure of the language, the thrill of its haunts, and the deliciously mordant laughter of ghouls."—Kyla Lee Ward, author of *The Macabre Modern and Other Morbidities*

"K. A. Opperman has been a dominant figure in the field of weird poetry. *Past the Glad and Sunlit Season* is a compelling volume from beginning to end."—S. T. Joshi

The Laughter of Ghouls

The Laughter of Ghouls

K. A. Opperman

Illustrated by Dan V. Sauer

Hippocampus Press

New York

Published by Hippocampus Press
P.O. Box 641, New York, NY 10156.
www.hippocampuspress.com

Interior illustrations, cover, and cover design by Daniel V. Sauer,
dansauerdesign.com.
Hippocampus Press logo designed by Anastasia Damianakos.

First Edition
1 3 5 7 9 8 6 4 2

ISBN 978-1-61498-328-6 paperback

Contents

I dedicate this book unto the Night herself.
May she forever enshroud my heart.

Introduction: Tainted Laughter

When I first set out to write this book, I had it in mind that I was going to try to write a collection of purely Gothic poetry. Such a book as I envisioned seemed to exist in the popular imagination—that crimson volume moldering on the shelves of a cavernous, raven-haunted study—and yet, outside of the collected poems of Poe, or perhaps *The Book of Jade,* by David Park Barnitz, there seemed to be no clear material counterpart for this romantic conception. So, realizing what appeared to be an obscure gap in poetic literature, I tried to write it.

In attempting to remain true to the classic Gothic tradition, I have populated the present volume with many of the familiar monsters and tropes of the genre—vampires, werewolves, witches, corpse-brides, ancient curses, lost loves, and the like. Some might say these are hackneyed themes, and perhaps they are, but I believe there are deep-rooted reasons why these themes have been explored and re-explored for centuries, and I have sought to revivify them. I have attempted to distill the most pure and perfect essence of these subjects, so that they may shine with renewed clarity in our modern age, freed from the obscuring fogs of antiquity.

Over the lengthy course of compiling this volume, toward the latter stages, ultimately, it was inevitable that I would stray slightly from the perhaps too-tight focus of my initial conception. A number of poems have been included that do not adhere strictly to the classic Gothic theme, among them quite a few poems of a folk-horror bent, as well as a slew of pieces that might more easily fit under the generic umbrella of the weird. In making these allowances, I was able to include virtually my entire poetic output since completing my first collection, *The Crimson Tome,* in 2015. Only my numerous poems pertaining to Halloween, as well as a small handful of others, have been omitted, to comprise future collections.

The volume in hand is divided into five thematic sections. The first section, "Graveyards Forgotten," contains poems concerning the corpse-plundering ghouls, as well as verses of a certain nocturnal aesthetic that also make mention of them. The second section, "Carpathian Spells," explores the vampiric superstitions of Transylvania and other related horrors. The third section, "Ghostly Sighs," covers a diverse selection of ghosts and phantoms. The fourth section, "Songs of the Goat," contains invocations, rites, odes, and other explorations of the sinistral. Finally, the fifth section, "Nightshade Flowers," examines misfits, freaks, grotesqueries, fantasies, and lovers divided by the yawning grave, thus completing a cycle begun—or ended—by the ravenous foraging of the ghouls.

The window is open, the curtains of crimson velvet flap in the night-wind, and the graveyard awaits. The crescent moon hangs above this darkest of nights like a harvest blade, and the ghouls' tainted laughter dances amid decaying leaves caught in the eternal sigh of autumn. Trust not the blood-red star Aldebaran; trust it not, but follow it, for it shall lead you aright, if it is nightmare you seek. Go, and receive the bloody kiss of the Nightmare Muse; she whose embrace is the dead moonlight itself; she whose long, trailing tresses are the shadows cast by raven-wings over ancient graves, and the all-enveloping blackness of oblivion.

Come—she is waiting for you.

—K. A. OPPERMAN

Corona, California
20 November 2019

The Laughter of Ghouls

Graveyards Forgotten

The Laughter of Ghouls

I have heard it of midnights, the laughter of ghouls,
On the winds that have strayed through my dreaming
As I nap in my armchair upholstered in gules,
By the window where shadows are teeming.

What a high, awful sound is the laughter I hear—
So exultant beneath the moon's crescent!
How I long through the forest autumnal and sere—
'Neath Aldebaran's beacon rubescent—

To go roam with the ghouls, to partake of their ways,
And to share in their hideous laughter!—
Would to God I could howl with the ghouls in the haze
Of the graveyard a charnel feast after . . . !

I have heard it of midnights, the laughter of ghouls,
And the night is not long in the coming
When my dream-driven body that gibbers and drools
Will go join them, to madness succumbing.

Ghoul Moon

When Luna's mad smile
Illumines the night—
A thing to beguile,
Her Crescent of white—
I hear in the forest
That mournfulest chorist
Who howls from the hoarest
Of tombs at her sight.

The nights of the Crescent
Are darkest by far,
And when erubescent
Shines Taurus' star,
The ghouls through a gloaming
Of witch-light are roaming,
The autumn woods combing,
Eternal and far.

With them I would wander
The dim lands of dream,
And slowly grow fonder
Of maidens that gleam
'Neath moonlight forever,
Their white eyelids never
To stir, nor to sever
Their lips' purple seam.

Ghoul Moon

In graveyards forgotten,
We'd plunder the tombs
Of monarchs long rotten;
From myrrh-scented glooms
We'd filch rubied chalice,
Wines crimson as malice,
In sepulcher palace
To toast to men's dooms.

Through woodland and hollow
Where glows the weird light
Of fungi I'll follow
Their howling aright—
When Luna's mad smile
Does gleam and beguile,
For mile on mile
Bewitching the night.

Among the Ghouls

By the moon's morbid beams,
Through a mist of dead dreams,
We were scavenging graves for fresh corses;
For upon the deceased
We would make nightly feast,
Frightened only by grave-robbers' horses.

Countless treasures we found
In the coffin-filled ground—
Withered roses and lovers' old lockets;
But these things we ignored
For our charnel reward,
And the maggots that squirmed in their sockets.

O to taste the white flesh
Of a maiden still fresh . . .
For a ghoul it were greatest of pleasures!—
Save perhaps to explore,
For a minute or more,
Every one of her soon-rotten treasures. . . .

By the moon's morbid beams,
Through a mist of dead dreams,
Being sated with feasting unhallowed,
We returned whence we came,
To a land with no name,
Yet another necropolis fallowed.

Woodland Funeral

My love lay dead upon her marble bier,
Amid the autumn forest red and sere,
Through which a wind of whispering spirits roamed.
It seemed a mourning sprite it was that combed
The crimson bough above her raven mane,
All flowing wide like some dark queen's black train,
To rain upon her hair an autumn crown—
A diadem of almandines. Her gown
Glowed ghostly white beneath the Huntress Moon,
Which like a silver mirror shared the swoon
Of death upon her fair, pale face, and lent
The starry luster of the firmament
To her dead eyes, which seemed alive with light,
Although they stared from out the utter night.
And as I bent to kiss her purple lips—
Perchance to drown my grief in the eclipse
Of one last passion—all the woodland ghouls
Began to howl and mourn their queen, who rules
Forevermore in perfect, pallid death,
With perfumed whispers on corruptless breath.

In Fits of Wildest Dreaming

In fits of wildest dreaming,
When demons all were teeming,
And scheming
To conquer midnight's throne,
I tossed in deepest slumber,
Through nightmares without number,
To cumber
The more, with awful groan,

My bed of silken scarlet.
A harpy-wingèd harlot—
A starlet
From courts of white Selene—
Seemed hellishly to hover
About me like a lover,
And cover,
With kisses so obscene,

My body, helpless sleeping!—
It seemed that she was reaping,
And keeping,
My soul with every kiss!
The succubus embraced me,
In ghostly beauty faced me,
To taste me,
And let me dream of bliss.

But there was scarce of pleasure,
No amorous red measure
To treasure,
Within my poisoned pulse;
For restless woes and worries
Swirled round me like lemures,
Or flurries
Of leaves that soon convulse

In graying autumn grasses,
As pensively there passes
Of lasses
The saddest of them all—
Poor Vespertina's specter,
When purple dusk has decked her,
Her nectar
Gone all to bitter gall.

And all the ghouls were howling,
The moonlit tombs befouling—
An owling
Made much of mournful moan—
When I was wildly dreaming,
And demons all were teeming,
And scheming
To conquer midnight's throne.

The Laughter of Ghouls

To Court the Night

It was at midnight, while the imp of Sleep
Yet frolicked with the sylphs beyond my grasp,
That I espied the blood-red book whose clasp
Was wrought of bronze, and then began to weep.

For was it not the fabled Crimson Tome
That I had once beheld in childhood dream?—
It lay upon my desk in doubtful gleam
Of sallow candles set against the gloam.

I had awaited this for fifty years—
To glimpse its haunted pages just one time!
So as the clock declared its thirteenth chime,
And daemons whispered madness in my ears,

I opened up the pretty clasp, and pored
Over vermillion verses eviler
And more diseased than I could then endure—
I howled for mercy and misericord . . . !

I heard the tainted laughter of the ghouls
Borne on the winds that through the window swirled
To strow dead leaves of autumn, sere and curled,
Upon the carpet, where strange pixy-stools

Began to fruit with foul fecundity
And sneer with half-formed faces—where the wild
Demesne of Nature had, I saw, defiled
My gloomy chamber's far profundity.

Nearly ensnared, I braved the ivy vines
That slithered past the threshold of the night
To clutch the claw-foot chairs—an aconite
Of primal nature spreading creeping tines

Of pagan poison through my home's warm heart!
I hurtled headlong through the window wide
Unto the Night, to court my darkling bride,
A victim of her necromantic art.

O Nightmare Muse! She of the long, dark hair!—
She of fair flesh, and poisoned apple lips!
She plied a pendulum of swaying hips,
Her sable gown whipped up on windy air.

Yes, I had seen her walking by the woods,
And so I hastened toward their gloomy verge;
A distant owl sang out its mournful dirge,
And somber monks, in ranks of brownish hoods,

Bore forth a coffin from a chapel carved
With evil gargoyles, which regarded them
With hungry grins, as if they would condemn
The precious corpse unto the ghouls long-starved.

To Court the Night

The hungry ghouls! I heard their laughter still,
And followed it among the clutching trees.
The scent of rot was strong upon the breeze—
Dead autumn leaves, exhumed cadavers chill.

The crescent moon ascended murky skies—
For night is darkest 'neath her silver horns;
Aldebaran, above the dream-held bourns,
Beamed like a crimson flame that slowly dies.

I came at last upon a graveyard gate,
Whose Gothic lacework ivy-overgrown
Hung just ajar, in nightshade breezes blown,
The iron hinges crying 'neath its weight.

A single lantern charmed the mist beyond,
And toward its ghostly light, I slowly passed
'Mid ruined graves gray weeds had over-grassed,
Upon whose plots disturbing mushrooms spawned.

A pack of ghouls dispersed at my approach—
Mere phantom shapes that roamed the greenish mist
In search of corpses whom decay had kissed,
The rotting province of the pestful roach.

The lantern shone upon an open grave,
And in the coffin's purple velvet slept
A pallid beauty waiting to accept
The adoration of a living slave.

I laid me down inside her lavish bed
To taste her lips, fair Proserpina's fruits;
In necrophilia's most proud pursuits
I would indulge, a lover of the dead.

But lo, her bosom held a heart's dim beat,
And from her mouth there stole a ghost of breath. . . .
Her lashes' fringed portcullis, closed on death,
Began to lift, her lilac lids replete

With promises of life ephemeral,
If only for a moment's romance doomed
Ere dawn of time. . . . But then some devil loomed
Above the grave, so fair, funereal.

And it was she, the Nightmare Muse, my queen,
Engowned in black, encrowned with cold, dead stars!
Her lips, a rose-bloom sapped with poison tars,
Promised a luscious kiss so deep, obscene,

And sensual that I could not resist
The promise of their cup, despite the pale
White-gownèd beauty waking from the dwale
Of death beneath me, cheeks now scarlet-kissed.

And so I turned to bid the girl goodbye—
But only saw a desiccated corpse
Afruit with that foul mushroom-cap which warps
The dreams of men, and drinks them when they die.

I heard the harlot's laughter on the air,
And from that fungus-drugged mirage I fled
Into the autumn woodlands filled with dread,
Aldebaran an orange, eternal glare.

Among the ghouls, toward that dream-ward star,
I stumbled on through Slumber's ebon gates,
After that black-gowned beauty who awaits
All foolish dreamers who dare dream too far.

Carpathian Spells

Transylvanian Darkness

The wolves howl out in primeval hunger;
The wind blows coldly, caressing
The red gown of a bride who for beauty had died
In the black, Transylvanian darkness.

By woodlands old when Time was much younger
I pace, forever obsessing
Over lost Nevermore, in this graveyard of yore
In the black, Transylvanian darkness.

The vampire plagues this province forsaken
By God and shunned by the village—
But my blood has grown chill, and my heart all but still,
In the black, Transylvanian darkness.

Blue flames on cursed Walpurgis awaken
Where lies old Dacian pillage,
But my treasure long lost fills a grave over-mossed
In the black, Transylvanian darkness.

A castle stands whose ruins will never
Forget a romance medieval . . .
Where the wild rose entwines under Luna's white tines
In the black, Transylvanian darkness.

Transylvanian Darkness

The Land Beyond the Forest forever
Enslaves my soul to its evil,
'Neath Carpathian spells in this hell of all hells,
In the black, Transylvanian darkness.

A Queen of Carpathia

O my belovèd, in your loveliness
I trace the shadow of an ancient queen
Who ruled a proud, Carpathian demesne
From out a castle lost in wilderness.
Dead pomp and splendor haunt your sapphire eyes,
And in your visage rouged with eglantine,
I note refinement of a monarchess;
Your sable mane the baser comb belies.

I see you leaning from a moonlit tower,
To catch cruel winter's kiss upon your cheek,
But why so mournful, I cannot surmise,
Nor why you watch the forest at that hour.
I only know that on that night antique,
The wolves all serve you, howling as they scour
Those haunted mountains, barren, cold, and bleak.

Portrait of the Countess

(An Acrostic)

Ensanguined by the blood of murdered girls,
Reclining nude within her crimson bath,
Zealously bathing, Erzsebet, whose wrath
Slew countless servants, tossed her raven curls.
Eyeing her fairness in a golden glass,
Bathory vowed to walk whatever path
Ended in deathless beauty. . . . Rubies, pearls—
These were mere baubles of the noble class.

Blood was more precious than these paltry things!
And sipping handfuls, soon did she surpass
The wonted redness of a woman's lips . . .
Her mouth the garnet-red that blood-thirst brings.
Over her breasts, and laving ivory hips,
Red flowed the vital wine, and visionings
Yearnful of fadeless youth did all eclipse.

Blood and Beauty

O Erzsebet, I offer up my blood
Unto your beauty—life is less to me
Than to behold your hair's black sheen, and see
Upon your fair white face a deeper rud.

Grant me but this—to glimpse within the pool
Of blood that flows from out my heart's deep wells,
As in a crimson mirror, all the spells
Of your appearance, beautiful and cruel.

O My Vampiress

For A. D.

I serve you, O my vampiress—
I spill my blood to paint your lips,
The while you twine one darkling tress
Around your pointed fingertips.

I serve you, O my sanguine queen,
A slave before your velvet throne.
Your glance of sapphire tinged with green
By candlelight has cruelly shone.

Symbols of Blood

Blood is the wine of your body, the burning and vibrant elixir.

Blood is the river of life that flows out of your vein.

Blood is the blossoming rose and the beautiful maiden that picks her.

Blood is the secret in scarlet, your joy and your pain.

The Black Czarina

The Black Czarina rules in Halycz castle,
The Gothic gem of all Galician lands;
In chambers draped with purple silk and tassel,
Her vixen servants wait her stern commands.

Without the arching window, Winter stretches
Its opal carpet toward Carpathia,
And as she spies its twilight woods, she catches
From plagueful winds vampiric mania. . . .

With jeweled boot upon her former master,
The very Czar, who serves her as a slave,
The pale blonde beauty proves a lustful caster
Of her black whip, to help the Czar behave.

He pours her wine, but spills the silver chalice—
And so she thinks to quaff a different wine. . . .
The scimitar comes down with all her malice,
To loose a font of torrid, ruby brine.

Before the nobles in her hall assembled,
She holds aloft their monarch's severed head:
With luscious lips that late for blood have trembled,
She kisses it, and stains her tongue blood-red.

—Loosely based on Leopold von Sacher-Masoch's "The Black Czarina"

The Vampire-Slayer's Whip

With aspergillum, sage, and prayer,
A sainted priest of old
Imbued this whip with blessings rare
To fight the Devil's fold.

For centuries it has been passed
Adown my family line,
And now it comes to me at last—
This destiny is mine.

From easternmost Germania,
I come to rid the land
Of devils Transylvania
Is plagued by, whip in hand.

A castle in Carpathia
Is where my foe awaits—
The crumbling Castle Dracula,
Of gargoyle-guarded gates.

And though it be Walpurgis eve,
When vampiresses pale
To kiss my neck so closely cleave
With lips of ruby bale,

I chase them off, and stay my course,
And flay whatever foe
From out the forest comes, remorse
A thing I do not know.

The wolves toward the silver horns
Of Luna lift their howls,
And nigh the woodland's goblin bourns
Blue fire the night befouls,

But holy purpose spurs me on
To slay the vampire pest,
Whose flesh were better touched by dawn
Than by this weapon blessed.

The Lady of the Dagger

The Lady of the Dagger
Had gorgeous chestnut locks;
Her ice-blue eyes could stagger
The fiercest foe that walks.

The dagger was enchanted,
A ruby-studded blade
To which a witch had chanted
Dread runes and darkly prayed.

The dagger woke the darkness
Within her human heart,
A coldness and a starkness,
A lust for battle's art.

She loved to draw its sparkling
Sharp silver down her neck
And ivory cleavage . . . darkling
Demeanor in her beck.

The foes that dared to face her
Went heartless to the grave;
The ravens all would chase her,
And hearts began to crave. . . .

Each victim was her lover,
For at the lethal thrust,
How near them she would hover,
And ply red lips in lust. . . .

Vampiric silver sated,
And slaked her dark desire,
When battle had abated,
She left them to the Fire.

The Lady of the Dagger
Forever roamed afar,
Wherever it would drag her,
Beneath a bloody star.

Empress of Vampires

She wears the moonlight for her maquillage,
And darkest kohl to shroud her olive eyes;
She almost seems to shimmer, a mirage
Amid the slumbrous blossoms' balmy sighs;
Her fanning ruff, a gemmy camouflage
Round chestnut tresses, is an orchid-bloom
Of ivory lace occulting mauvy skies.

Her slender fingers grasp a pale pink rose
Adorned with blood-drops spilt from parted lips;
Her enigmatic gaze, her pensive pose—
Beneath a crescent moon so near eclipse—
Suggest the weight of more-than-mortal woes;
While her black dress, the vestment of the tomb,
Curves out to veil her cold and childless hips.

Carmilla

Carmilla, Carmilla, this castle is lonely,
The Styrian twilight is fraught with despair;
Carmilla, Carmilla, my one and my only,
Do come and let down your abundant brown hair. . . .

Carmilla, Carmilla, the full moon is rising
Above the dark forest where revenants roam;
Carmilla, Carmilla, there is no disguising
My awe of your beauty this mystical gloam.

Carmilla, Carmilla, I still can remember
The night your black carriage was wrecked by that tree. . . .
Carmilla, Carmilla, the subtlest ember
Was lit in my heart at your intimacy!

Carmilla! Carmilla! a shadow of horror
Did flit through my soul when I first saw your face!
Carmilla! Carmilla! my midnight adorer
From when I was six, whom no years would erase!

Carmilla, Carmilla, your beauty soon won me—
Your long, tangled tresses, your milky-white skin. . . .
Carmilla, Carmilla, you could have undone me,
Your amorous glances nigh drove me to sin.

Carmilla! Carmilla! your dangerous languor
Begins to ensnare me, so fatal, your touch!
Carmilla! Carmilla! the terrible clangor
That beats from my heart in your soft, silken clutch . . . !

Carmilla! Carmilla! your kisses are cleaving
Too hotly upon your dear Laura's cool cheek!
Carmilla! Carmilla! your bosom is heaving—
Your breath is so stifling—I'm growing so weak!

Carmilla! Carmilla! in dream something pricked me
Upon my left breast on this fresh purple spot!
Carmilla! Carmilla! please tell me you tricked me—
Your mouth and white gown with fresh blood all ablot!

Carmilla! Carmilla! there lurks a strange danger—
A monstrous black cat prowled my room in the night!
Carmilla! Carmilla! trust not any stranger—
A vampire fear sweeps the land like a blight!

Carmilla! Carmilla! why won't you acknowledge
Whenever I knock in the small, midnight hours?
Carmilla! Carmilla! can mandrake or smallage
Compel your weird sleep-walks in moon-bathèd bowers . . . ?

Carmilla! Carmilla! you mimic this painting
Of Countess Mircalla so awfully well!
Carmilla! Carmilla!—I feel near to fainting—
The cursed race of Karnstein so long ago fell. . . .

—After J. Sheridan Le Fanu's "Carmilla"

Clarethea

As I survey this violet-misted vale
From this my castle in Carpathia,
I think of only my Clarethea,
Who in despair leapt from this balcon-rail.

The wolves that howl within the woods below
Raise for Clarethea their canine rune—
Nay, nevermore unto the wan full moon
Shall they address their wild and ancient woe!

I watch the phantom of her funeral
Procession pass along the lonely road;
They bear Clarethea to death's abode;
Their torches flare in twilight mystical.

This very eve it was, a twelvemonth flown,
That my Clarethea was laid to rest
In her ancestral tomb—the storied nest
Of deathless vampires, as we well had known.

She often haunts this crumbling balcony,
The pallid specter of Clarethea;
And when the sun sets on Carpathia
Will I await her, freed from misery.

Clarethea

Whether my love, or devil, on this eve
I go to be with her forevermore—
Clarethea! love whom I most adore!
For you all life and light I fain would leave.

I hear the distant tolling of the bell
The village chapel rings at vesper-time—
For fair Clarethea they sound the chime,
And for my death they sound the doomful knell.

This is my final sunset, this, my last,
And ever after, the eternal night.
Clarethea! my bride, my starry-bright!
We are together in the golden past.

The Woman in the Feathered Mask

I met a woman at the masquerade
Who wore a feathered mask
With midnight plumes of ravens all arrayed,
And laced-up sable basque.

Down pallid shoulders spilled her copper locks;
Her lips were apple red;
With enigmatic greenish eyes, the fox
My footsteps toward her led.

We shared a dance beneath the chandelier,
We shared a sinful kiss—
I did not like the masks that circled near,
As if to witness this.

With ivory tooth she bit my ravished lip,
And licked the bloody drop—
In sudden fear, I ran from out her grip,
And did not dare to stop.

An open window proved my one escape—
I leapt from off its ledge
Into the darkness, tearing crimson drape,
And landing in a hedge.

I stumbled through the moonlit garden, rent
By thorns of roses white,

Until my blood unto their blooms had lent
Red dew like rubies bright.

But I was stopped upon the petaled track
As by a baleful spell—
I turned to see the beauty dressed in black,
The dance's darkling belle.

For she observed me from a balcony,
And gave the Evil Eye!
I held aloft the cross I kept on me,
Then through the night did fly.

I dreamt she pressed against the window-pane
Her pale and yielding skin,
Imploring me in whispered sweet refrain
To please, please let her in.

She was completely naked, save her mask,
And kindled my desire.
I threw the casement wide, as if to bask
In moonlight's icy fire.

She drifted inward, borne on scarlet mist,
And clomb into my bed. . . .
It was my neck that she most fiercely kissed—
She licked and sucked it red.

But when I woke from out an awful swoon,
The maskèd nymph had gone.
I was alone with Artemis' moon,
Her crescent bow full-drawn.

Alone I say, but for the great black bird
That watched from just outside—
A stately raven, saying not a word
As night-wind sadly sighed.

But all at once, the watchful bird took flight—
Toward the looming manse
Where I had tarried on one haunted night
In masquer's dreamful dance.

And then I knew that I must soon return
To that accursèd place—
For I was sick, and how my soul did burn
Just once to see her face!

I traveled there at even, for the sun
Seemed brighter than its wont;
Now purple palls of shadow had begun
The autumn woods to haunt.

I was aware that I was followed by
A flock of silent crows;
They rustled darkly in the dusking sky
Of daylight's plaintive close.

I was compelled by some nocturnal power
To seek again that garth
Wherein there grew a sometimes sanguine flower
With roots in Satan's hearth.

Hid in a bower, I beheld the gleam
Of marble in the gloom—

A mausoleum caught the final beam
Of daylight's flaming doom.

I entered in, descending well-worn stairs
By Gothic sconces lit;
The candles flickered like to sickly flares
As deeper delved the pit.

I came into a chamber chill and dim,
And on a dais laid,
I found the fairest of the seraphim
In perfect sleep displayed.

She lay inside a coffin finely lined
With velvet bright vermeil,
But still her face was half concealed behind
That raven-feathered veil!

With cautious hand, I sought to take the mask
From off her placid face—
For ere I staked her bosom, I would bask
In her uncovered grace!

But just as I had brushed one sable plume,
The crows came rushing in,
And all their raucous cawing in that tomb
Made such a frightful din!

Her lashes fluttered in the candlelight—
She threatened to awake!
No precious second could I spare this night
If I the curse would break!

I drove the stake between her ivory breasts,
To pierce her vampire heart—
And doing so, the empress of the pests
So violently did start!

She screamed in horror, clutching at the stake,
And pulled it from her flesh—
And then in mocking, long red nails did rake
Her bosom healed afresh!

And yet the deadly wound had struck its mark
Unto her rotten core—
Consumed in flame, she went unto the dark
To rest forevermore.

Amid the sighing ashes that remained,
There only lay her mask,
Whose hidden visage I had never gained—
Ill-starred had been the task.

And yet my dreams are often haunted by
A ghostly, gorgeous face
When I have kissed her raven mask, and hie
To moonlit dreams' embrace.

Roses, Black Roses

The darkness becomes her,
She wears it for gown;
Oblivion numbs her
From toe unto crown
Of roses, black roses—
Her dreams all but drown
In rot-tainted perfume,
Dead moths that fall down.

The darkness becomes her,
This marble-white belle,
Who mournfully hums her
Strange song, 'neath the spell
Of roses, black roses,
Whose kiss cannot quell
Her lips pained with perfume
Of blood bought in hell.

Bloody Tears

In that forgotten Gothic chapel, pale and pained,
A carven angel in an alcove stood.
I placed my taper in her cuppèd hands, and gained
View of her visage weeping tears of blood.

"Wherefore these bloody tears?" I asked her, sad of heart.
"A prayer that your weeping find surcease!
Would that your sad, seraphic lips could come apart
And speak to me of what disturbs your peace."

Whereat a matronly and melancholy voice
Wailing awoke from out her tortured stone.
Here was a miracle, yet I did not rejoice
At what the statue told with many a moan:

"I weep because the gargoyles, guardians of this place,
Have wicked grown beneath an evil moon.
I weep because the witch and devil oft disgrace
These holy grounds, adance on flaming shoon.

I weep because vampires usurp the pulpit here,
Preaching their crimson sermon drop by drop.
I weep because deep poisons well up tear by tear,
Which cold, unclosing eyelids cannot stop."

Eventide

When violet turns the eventide,
A revenant is seen to glide
Along the haunted woodland wide,
Diaphanous and pale.

The silver stars of even crown
The ghostly tulle that serves to gown
Her body from the brow and down,
Bare curves beneath the veil.

The bats attend her silken train,
And hover round her raven mane.
She hungers for a living vein
On lifeblood's beating trail.

When violet turns the eventide,
Beware the crimson-mouthèd bride,
For many men have gladly died
To fill her sanguine grail.

Queen of the Bats

Upon her moonlit tower,
All naked to the night,
A wan and wicked flower,
She bids the bats alight.

Proffering scarlet nectar,
She raises up her wrist;
The flapping bats collect her
Hot ichor as they list.

Her blood inside them beating,
The bats obey their queen;
They swarm in monstrous meeting
Above her wild demesne.

They feed on fairest women
Who brave the village gloam,
Till mortal lanterns dimmen
In shadow of her home.

Queen of the Bats

The Harpy

She came on wings of scarlet,
The harpy pale and fair,
To tempt my dark-haired Charlotte—
O maiden rathe and rare!
Now I have but this starlit
Escarpment and despair.

She came on wings of scarlet
While restlessly we slept—
For now a wicked starlet
Upon the sky had crept—
Most red of stars that are lit,
Which hell would not accept!—

She came on wings of scarlet,
But scarce was I awake
When, hand in hand, the harlot
My spellbound bride did take
Unclothed upon the scar lit
By moonlight . . . crimson rake!

The fiend with wings of scarlet
Embraced my bride above
The valley from afar lit
By haunted stars whereof
Still tell the wails of Charlotte—
My lost and fallen love!

The Hunter and the Succubus

He sauntered through the swinging door,
A tarnished pistol held in hand;
He sought their most bewitching whore,
Renowned across the land.

The madam smiled, matriarch
Of crimson women infamous,
But in the brothel's scarlet dark,
He sought the succubus.

The hunter leveled silver death
Toward the ladies waiting there;
The room grew warm with perfumed breath,
And scented with their hair.

Among them was a devil-girl,
A demon-human masquerade,
But whether decked in gem or pearl,
He knew not how arrayed.

He held his flashing crucifix
Toward the harlots' laughing band;
The parlor grew as dark as Styx
Around its image grand.

A ghostly redhead softly hissed,
And shied into a shadowed hall;

One second gone, and lead had kissed
Her shadow on the wall.

He chased her up the narrow stair,
Into a bedroom ready-made:
Red curtains flapped on open air—
A clever game she played.

He bounded from the balcony,
And landed on his trusted steed;
Though cunning as a falcon, she
In flight would not succeed.

Thick elf-locks curled the creature's mane,
And hell-coals lit her fiery eyes;
And from her crown a wicked twain
Of horns were seen to rise.

This was a monster, not his horse—
And off she took him, furious.
She thundered down a tortured course,
The ride delirious.

At last he steered her toward the church,
And crashed her through the oaken door;
Across the font she came to lurch,
The hunter on the floor.

She tumbled in the holy bath,
Transforming back to human form;
All wet and wanton in her wrath,
She perished in a storm.

When Wolfsbane Blooms

When wolfsbane blooms,
And coldly looms
The death-white winter moon,
The purest man
Carpathian
Dark spells will peril soon.

Who nears the wort
That leaves amort
The wolves that eat its leaves,
On certain nights
Will meet the wights
Of wolves the forest grieves.

They prowl around
The flower crowned
With baleful bluish hoods,
The wraiths of wolves,
Where mist convolves
With devil-haunted woods.

They will possess,
At one caress
Of wolfsbane's fatal flower,
Those foolish men
Who cannot ken
Carpathia's dark power.

And thus is born,
Ere come of morn,
The Werewolf—feared of all
Who dwell beneath
The savage teeth
Of eastern mountains tall.

When wolfsbane blooms,
And coldly looms
The death-white winter moon,
The wolf in man
Carpathian
Dark spells will waken soon.

Werewolf

The full moon is rising
From out the red trees,
Dead branches disguising
Its leprous disease;
The Wolf is now rising
Within, realizing
My curse, my disease,
This mournful, accursed autumn night.

I howl to my brothers—
Wolves answer my call;
Town maidens and mothers
Pray rosary, all.
The townsmen, my brothers
By day, are now Others—
Amassing, they all
Hold pitchforks and torches alight.

I prowl through the woodland
Outside of the town—
A ghoulish, ungood land
Where wan flowers drown.
Dark mere of the woodland,
O what visage should land
Here?—would it would drown!—
A wolf-face of crimson-eyed fright!

I tear though their torches,
Their pitchforks I snap!
Slay men on their porches,
Their bright blood to lap!
A fallen torch torches
A house, the town scorches!
Her blood I would lap—
That maiden all moonlight-bedight!

I sweep up the maiden
With one savage arm,
An angel of Aidenn
Who screams in alarm.
I kidnap the maiden,
My claws sweetly laden—
The bell sounds alarm!
I carry her off, out of sight.

I fly through the forest,
The tolling grows far.
I head for the hoarest
Of hills, for a Star
Rules over the forest
This night of my sorest
Of trials! and the Star
Can challenge the moon's awful might.

Surrounded by roses
That ruins entwine,
She sleeps in sprawled poses—

I see her for mine!
This lily 'mid roses,
Who tomb-top reposes—
She always was mine!
I lust her white beauty to bite. . . .

The moon becomes veiled
By curtains of cloud;
The Star has not failed,
So silvery proud!
The Man lately veiled
By evil ungaoled,
I weep here, unproud,
Above my beloved's cold wight.

Her white eyelids waken
Beneath the Star's rays!
My Faith has been shaken—
Now seraphs I praise!
But though she awaken,
Forever forsaken,
I sing my sad praise,
Her love nevermore to requite.

Wilhelmina

There was a torch to light the gloom—
The gloom that clotted every room
Within that ivy-chainèd manse—
Her name was Wilhelmina!

Her green eyes pierced me like a lance—
A lance thrown with the surest stance!
But never looked she long as I
At her, my Wilhelmina.

When candelabrum flickered nigh—
Shone nigh enough to aid my eye—
I marked how ghostly, lily-fair
Was my dear Wilhemina!

And marked I too that red-gold hair!—
That hair that framed her haunting stare,
And curled upon the bosom proud
Of precious Wilhelmina!

These charms with which she was endowed—
Endowed divinely!—from a shroud
Of gloom I studied, quickly caught
In the spell of Wilhelmina!

But her sole suitor I was not—
Was not the only guest that sought
The favor of the Baron's child—
New-blossomed Wilhelmina!

The gala-guests all danced and smiled—
But smiled I not as suitors filed
Around to kiss the jeweled hand
Of my—my Wilhelmina!

The viol-screech I could not stand—
Nor stand could I—nor understand—
The harsh, high laughter all awhirl
Around pure Wilhelmina!

They saw me then—I watched the girl—
The girl who with them felt unfurl
My ire, my passion, my mad love
For shining Wilhelmina!

They gathered round my shadowed cove—
The cove wherein I'd hoped to prove
In private my devotion to
My lovèd Wilhelmina.

The ladies 'mid them drained of hue—
In hue the men blanched slightly, too;
But one among them came to fore—
Angelic Wilhelmina!

Our gazes met like never before!
Before she'd only glanced—no more;
But now she *stared,* and breathed so near—
My love, *my* Wilhelmina!

She formed a smile quaint and queer—
How *queer!* But—she embraced me dear!
How close that long-evanished night
When I knew Wilhelmina!

Upstairs she took me, holding tight—
So tight!—till gloom hid us from sight.
Her fingers curled around my frame—
The touch of Wilhelmina!

Into a sconce-lit hall we came,
Then came where armor-suits might maim
Trespassers in the Baron's home—
Save I and Wilhelmina!

Through hallways' sempiternal gloom—
A gloom flame-starrèd—did we roam,
Till came we to a huge arched door
Which oped for Wilhelmina.

Inside, a vast storehouse of lore!—
Old lore, in bindings bound of yore.
Led was I past cold, moldy books,
Clasped by warm Wilhelmina!

We ducked through dim, disheveled nooks—
Quaint nooks, through which we crept like crooks.
But paramours we really were—
Me and sweet Wilhelmina!

What book she plucked I was unsure—
Unsure, for I was watching *her*!
But lo! a passage blackly yawned
For me and Wilhelmina!

We braved the stifling black beyond—
Beyond *all!*—guided by the wand
She held—for such the candle seemed
When held by Wilhelmina!

When round and up we went, I deemed—
This deemed—we clomb—unless I dreamed?—
The manor's ancient prison tower—
Me and brave Wilhelmina!

At that strange moonless, midnight hour—
An hour bewitched by some weird power—
We came to a bar-windowed cell—
Me and wild Wilhelmina!

A levin-flash illumed it well—
Too well!—my vanished friends did dwell
Within that high, forgotten room
To which came Wilhelmina!

All leaned against the wall, in gloom—
A gloom as cobwebbed as the tomb!
My friends who'd once hung in the Hall
All leered at Wilhelmina!

She propped me up to face the wall—
This wall where poison spiders crawl.
"You are most hideous of all!"
Quoth my love—Wilhelmina!

Ghostly Sighs

Amorella

Now wanton Amorella
Was peering in her mirror:
She drew toward it, nearer,
Her heart the tarantella
Of lust so madly dancing
As she undressed, entrancing
The priestess of Capella
That smiled at Amorella.

Enwreathed in dying roses,
Her mirror framed a demon,
Whom she would claim for leman—
A nymph whose Sapphic poses
Did mimic her example,
And pallid bosom ample;
Gold ringlets, one supposes
Of seraphs; lips like roses.

Quite perfect, her reflection—
Quite faithful, save one feature:
Two horns only a creature
Of dreamful, dark affection
Would have encrowned its tresses,
A midnight demoness'—
Yet still, she craved connection
Unto her fair reflection. . . .

She pressed with all her passion
Against the argent, rigid,
Flat surface nigh to frigid
Against her flesh, in fashion
Of amorous embracing,
Her tongue wet lust there tracing. . . .
She wished that she could smash in
This wall that barred her passion.

Pressed breast to breast, she gazed in
Brown eyes beneath long lashes—
Yet, strange, no more the clashes
Of glass she was enmazed in
Against her teeth kept kisses
From plumbing lips' abysses. . . .
It seemed she was enhazed in
The foggy glass she gazed in.

At last did Amorella
Embrace her mimic lover,
But only to discover
The wicked Cinderella—
Each secret recess tasted,
And all of love-wails wasted—
Had locked her in a cell, a
Glass cage for Amorella.

The Laughter of Ghouls

The Lady in Scarlet

The Lady in Scarlet
That castle does haunt,
A raven-haired deviless fair,
Dressed red as a harlot,
Who often does flaunt
Her charms from a balcony there.

Her delicate cincture
With diamonds adorned
Her fingers are fain to untie. . . .
Her silks of the tincture
Of blood are soon scorned,
To slip down white shoulder and thigh. . . .

O look not upon her
Pale flesh, her fair form
That puts even Lilith to shame!—
Who looks is a goner,
Entranced as a swarm
Of rose-vines come slowly to claim.

The days are as hours
To those she enthralls,
Who sleepily reach for their queen. . . .
Enfettered in flowers,
No skeleton falls,
Caught ever in crimson and green.

The Lady in Scarlet

Midnight in the Ebon Rose Bower

Why am I waking at this witchful hour?—
What succubus enspells with such a power
As to beguile this ebon-rosèd bower?

I glimpse her nymphish form upon the air,
A demoness mysterious and fair—
A scarlet perfume-specter, starlight-rare.

The roses whisper with their sleepy lips
Black phantasies. . . . The dew like diamonds drips
From petals played with by her swaying hips. . . .

I ache to clutch her in nocturnal lust,
But I am thwarted as the burning gust
Of my own breath dispels her haunted dust.

Absinthia

She comes to me from out the emerald gloom
That gathers in the shadows of my room,
When I am nodding, drunk with sharp perfume—
The breath of absinthe from my crystal glass.

She is a languid, strange, smaragdine girl,
Whose verdant tresses flowingly unfurl.
Pale sprigs of mugwort weave her crown, and curl
Around bare arms that beck from dream's morass.

Her mouth of wormwood—ah, her bitter kiss!—
Delivers me into the green abyss.
Upon her bosom's herby couch, the bliss
Of poisonous nepenthe fills my soul.

And yet Absinthia so soon is gone,
And in the liquor's cloudy celadon,
I see a sad reflection, worn and wan—
A ghoulish thing deformed by time's grim toll.

The Lady of the Graves

Who mourns the long departed,
Whom no salvation saves?
It is the mournful-hearted
Dark Lady of the Graves.

Whose kiss makes red each marker
On ways the tombstone paves?
No dress than hers is darker—
The Lady of the Graves.

Her wan and lace-veiled weeping
The ivied granite laves.
Red roses there are heaping—
Sweet Lady of the Graves!

Her black-beglovèd fingers
Caress what death engraves
On stone that coldly lingers,
Dear Lady of the Graves.

I almost think I love her,
She who grim gargoyles braves,
With Dian's horns above her!—
Good Lady of the Graves!

I pray that when I perish,
Where silver willow waves,
My memory she'll cherish—
My Lady of the Graves.

A Ghostly Lily

I came so softly stealing in the night,
To where my love lay slumbrous, beautiful,
Encrowned with dreams. . . . I stood there, dutiful,
As any lover at her bedside might.
The autumn moonlight icy made her face,
And every breath sent flowers of mist aflight—
But in her blood the life was bountiful;
It bloomed in roses from her heart's red vase.

O how I ached to kiss her just one time!
—And yet I knew my touch were instant death.
I stood beside her, played with bits of lace—
Yet I could not then harvest in its prime
The Rose of Life. One blossom from her breath,
A ghostly lily wrought of mist and rime,
Is all I reaped from my fair Ashtoreth.

The Shadow of the Reaper

I saw the Reaper in his purple robe
Reflected in my wineglass yesternight:
His grinning death's-head gleamed a ghastly white,
His bony hand reached forth my soul to probe.

I turned to face that grim dark angel, Death—
But there was naught behind me but the drapes
Of dull red velvet, forming dreadful shapes
As they did stir in night-wind's cold, black breath. . . .

I tried to hide among the gala guests
That danced beneath the crystal chandelier—
And yet between two lovers drawing near,
Again I glimpsed the Reaper, Lord of Pests.

He fixed me with his icy, eyeless gaze,
And held aloft in one decrepit hand
A wingèd hourglass, whose emblackened sand
Had nearly drained the dregs of all my days!

Now all the gladsome guests have gone, and I—
I am alone. The darkness closes in,
And in the gloom I see a graveyard grin
With rotted teeth, and roaches in each eye.

The Shadow of the Reaper

The booming chimes of midnight sound my doom—
The shadow of his scythe is on the wall,
And like the clock-hand's slow yet certain fall—
It lowers over harvest for the tomb!

The Spectral Knight

He stood upon a rotting bridge
All vague with ghostly fog,
Where never hummed the swarming midge,
And never sang the frog.

Just where this was I do not know—
But through the woodland wide
I'd wandered long through autumn's woe,
With silence at my side.

The spectral knight said none shall pass—
He spoke with rasping breath
That I should go and love my lass
Instead of courting death.

But I was mad with black despair,
And swiftly drew my sword
To slay the knight that waited there
The somber bridge to ward.

I stepped upon the haunted planks—
But O, the icy chill
That rose from off the riverbanks,
And seemed my heart to still!

The Spectral Knight

My limbs grew numb and slumberous,
And barely would obey;
My weapon seemed so ponderous
Amid the dreadful fray.

And soon I knelt in sore defeat,
A sword unto my heart—
And yet the knight did not complete
The victor's wonted part.

He bid me go and love my lass,
And savor living breath,
For soon, too soon, he'd let me pass
Into the land of death.

The Ghost Carriage

A ghostly carriage rides down lonely roads
On autumn nights like these,
When whippoorwills and owls and witch's toads
Sing mournful symphonies.

A pair of sable stallions pulls the car,
But driver there is none;
And through the wine-red drapes that parted are,
There peers a skeleton.

O there is room for one more passenger
Upon this haunted ride—
So seems to say the grinning messenger
From out the carriage-side.

When you are weary, lost, and wandering
One twilight long from now,
Perchance again you will be pondering
That car, with sorrowed brow.

Her Ghostly Sigh

Her pleading whispers stir the starlit drapes,
Through which the candles' spectral breath escapes.
O I have heard it when the candles die—
Her ghostly sigh.

Benighted roses wilt beneath her breath
As she returns from shadowed lands of death.
O how she begs me by her grave to lie—
Her ghostly sigh.

She haunts the garden in her wedding-gown—
O my belovèd, whom the lilies crown!
Tonight I heed my final lullaby—
Her ghostly sigh.

Soon I shall take her cold, white hand in mine,
Whereon a tarnished golden ring does shine,
And I shall go with her, untroubled by
Her ghostly sigh.

The Lady in White

I saw the lady gowned in white,
How ghostly white was she;
I met her of an autumn night,
Upon the misty lea.

A sorrow weighed upon her brow,
A sadness dimmed her eyes,
But she was lovely, I avow,
As Luna in the skies.

Her kiss was chilly on my cheek,
And cold her hand in mine
As through the woods we went to seek
Mnemosyne's dim shrine.

We found at last a sylvan grove,
And 'mid the autumn drift
A skeleton was interwove,
With mushrooms in each rift.

I turned to see her tearful face—
And yet the girl had gone,
Her spirit in its resting place
At scarlet crack of dawn.

And so I left her there to rest,
Beloved forevermore
Beneath the autumn leaves, where nest
The gnome and mandragore.

Songs of the Goat

Invocation of Diana

(Inspired by the painting "Diana" by Jules Joseph Lefebvre)

Diana, I pray you, descend
From out your sidereal court
Your pallid, strange passion to lend,
With knowledge of witchcraft and wort—
Diana, I pray you, descend!

O splendorous Queen of the Moon,
Whose brow bears the crescented tiar—
The horns that uprear through the swoon
Of dream and that glow like white fire!—
O splendorous Queen of the Moon!

Descend on the stairs of the stars,
On steps all of moonlight and mist,
Bare limbs like the palest of spars,
Red tresses by Vesper Star kissed—
Descend on the stairs of the stars!

Your marble, immaculate feet,
Diana, I pray you to place
On ground—for a Goddess unmeet!—
This violet-grown greensward to grace—
Your marble, immaculate feet!

O huntress, take up your great bow,
And lead, with the stag as your guide,
To woodlands no mortal may know,
Whose trees ancient wisdom confide.
O huntress, take up your great bow!

Diana, I pray you, descend
From out your sidereal court
Your pallid, strange passion to lend,
With knowledge of witchcraft and wort—
Diana, I pray you, descend!

Divinity

For A. D.

Divinity, my love, a silver flame,
Burns in your ancient, marble-carven breast.
Your mortal form is but a palimpsest;
Artemis, Ishtar, Luna, is your name.
A spectral crescent horns your raven hair,
Which only poets can but faintly see.
I bow before your lunar brilliancy,
Pierced by the vesper stars that haunt your stare.

O daughter of the Goddess many-formed—
Of moon and night, and witchcraft wrought by dusk—
Raise up your athame to moonlit sky,
And with the might that once within you stormed,
Rethroned amid a woman's worthy husk,
Call down the secrets of the stars on high.

Ode to Ashtoreth

For David Park Barnitz

O Ashtoreth, O perfect corpse-wan queen,
O Goddess gowned in glimmers of the moon,
O shining eyes half-shut in silver swoon,
I set your crown with what white gems men glean
From out the stars; I send you perfumed praise
Upon a golden censer's breath, so soon
Extinguishèd. . . . I fain would die between
Your deathly breasts, thereon to end my days.

For I have seen you in my love's fair face—
She who lies cold beneath the moon's blue rays!
And I have kissed on her corrupt pale lips
Your poppied lips; in hers, known your embrace.
O Ashtoreth, pray pity him who sips
From out your down-tipped opaled cup—I chase
Upon my love's cold breast the last eclipse.

Flame-Mistress of the Morning Star

Innana, Ishtar, Ashtoreth,
O rose-lipped lady pale as death;
Astarte, Artemis, Selene,
Horned huntress and the heavens' queen;
Diana, Juno Lucina,
With gold-girt thighs from Cythera;
And Luna Lucifera are
Flame-Mistress of the Morning Star.

Lilith

(After the painting "Lilith" by John Collier)

A dusky serpent wraps your pallid skin
As your dim eyelids close in ecstasy;
Your vermeil mouth curves up so temptingly,
And do you smile, O Lilith, queen of sin?

You take such pleasure in the snake's caress
While tossing back your hair of cinnabar.
O Lilith, Daughter of the Even Star,
Your flesh is purpled by the Serpent's press.

The Laughter of Ghouls

Lucia

Midwinter witch, the icy season's bride,
You who are gowned as with the virgin snow,
O Lucia the golden, lend your glow
This darkest day when all of light has died!

Six holy candles crown your flaxen locks,
Set in a wreath of verdant evergreen;
A scarlet sash, the cincture of a queen,
Surrounds your waist, you who in darkness walks.

And though your empty sockets weep red tears,
And a gold plate displays your plucked blue orbs,
You know the way; hibernal night absorbs
Your light in vain—a spark of hope appears!

So while the Wild Hunt sweeps through woodland snow,
And Mistress Winter casts her icy spell,
O Lucia, while clangs the argent bell,
Dispel our darkness, lend your holy glow!

Child of Ice

For A. D.

Born near the shortest day, the longest night,
While yet the Holly King maintains his throne,
You are a child of ice, the Winter's own,
Born of the darkness, knowing naught of light.

You raise your antlers at the feast of Yule,
Your chestnut tresses all with holly crowned,
And while Cernunnos roams the frozen ground,
Your blue eyes brighten, each a flame-lit jewel.

In the Dead of Winter

In the darkest dead of winter,
On the longest night of the year,
See the Yuletide fires of our long-dead sires
On the haunted hill appear.

In the barren dead of winter,
When the boughs are bare of leaf,
See the mistletoe on the gray oaks grow
Like a plague with no relief.

In the frozen dead of winter,
When the snow has whitened all,
See the Wild Hunt ride through the woodland wide
With a Horned God riding tall.

In the very dead of winter,
Turn your heart toward cheer and song—
For the dark was old ere the light unrolled,
And the night is very long.

Krampus

A grim and goatish devil,
Old Krampus is his name,
Has come to dim the revel
Beside the Christmas flame.

His scarlet tongue a-lolling,
A switch in shackled hand,
While Yuletide bells are tolling,
He roams the frozen land.

He stuffs his cumbrous basket
With those who've not been nice.
Now someone has to ask it:
Was mischief worth the price?

To hell the monster takes them,
Across the moonlit snow;
Saint Nicholas forsakes them—
Poor children lost below . . . !

On darkest Christmas Even,
If on your twinkling tree
You should forget to weave in
The angels' argentry,

Old Krampus comes to visit,
And takes his devil's due.
A ghostly tale, or is it?—
I tell you, it is true.

Priestess of the Goat

Priestess of the Goat

A snow-white skull with curling horns
Encrowns her black and lustrous hair;
She walks beyond by the twilight bourns
Of woods where Satan makes his lair.

Her velvet robe reveals her breasts
As branches snag the scarlet cloth;
Most favored of the Devil's guests,
She's fair as Ishtar-Ashtaroth.

Capella's yellow beacon guides
Her onward toward the Witches' Goat;
The sable beast in her confides
Black secrets she can never quote.

Beneath the cloven crescent moon,
They madly dance around the fire;
The Priestess sweetly wails the rune
Of an unspeakable desire. . . .

Chant of the Priestess

Satan, I will sing your praise,
Even as the silver rays
Of the lovely Even Star
Shine at twilight, near and far.

Satan, I will walk with you,
Naked as the witches do,
Through the black and brambled wood,
In a bloody sisterhood.

Satan, I will be your queen,
Mistress of your wild demesne,
Bounding on a sable goat
Through the mushroomed realms remote.

Satan, I will sign your book,
As you wait with cowl and crook
While I sign my crimson name,
Maiden of damnation's flame.

Song of the Goat

I have whispered in a witch's ear
All the secrets that she yearned to hear;
O'er the darkling hedge my hooves leap clear,
When the crescent moon holds reign.

I have suckled at her buxom teat,
Drinking moon-white milk till past replete;
I have felt her sighs of scarlet heat
As she strokes my night-black mane.

I have wandered through the woods at dusk,
Drinking in the autumn's deathly musk.
Many names are mine; I shed this husk
When the sabbat-fires burn bright.

I have pranced amid the shepherd's flock,
Made the chaste their silver belts unlock.
Ere the holy crowing of the cock,
Sign my book by candlelight.

Woods at Dusk

I wander through the woods at dusk,
The Devil walking by my side,
When Luna, crowned with twiform tusk,
Ascends, the vesper's bride.

The shadows deepen, Night awakes
In sylvan groves undelved by Day;
'Mid moss and gloom, my soul forsakes
The sun's last scarlet ray.

The Goat of Walpurgis

(After the painting "The Witches' Sabbath" by Francisco Goya)

The great black goat rears up its horns
Upon Walpurgis Eve,
To hail the crescent that adorns
The welkin spells to weave.

An oaken wreath encrowns its brow,
And bats converge above,
As naked witches wail and bow
To win the Devil's love.

Walpurgis Eve

The crickets chirp their plaintive tune
To charm the mystic afternoon,
While through the amber mist the moon
Gleams wanton, wild, and white.

The faeries dance their roundelays,
Glimpsed only by the vagrant gaze
That scans the flowered field where haze
Of dreams enchants the sight.

When twilight falls the witches ride
Their brooms to sabbats far and wide,
Each one to be a devil's bride
And dance around the fire.

They skip around the sickly flames,
All naked, shrieking ancient names.
A goat-god, Master of the Games,
Foul offspring soon will sire.

The Crimson Circle

The Puppet Master traced the rune
In red upon the scroll;
Beneath the pale Walpurgis moon,
He sold his very soul.

The Bearded One an unction dripped
Upon the doubtful Sign;
In palsied hand he tightly gripped
The Devil-got design.

The Poet spoke an evil verse
The talisman to taint—
An incantation nigh a curse,
Concerning witch and haint.

At last, the Priestess on the pyre
Did lay the paper square
To burn amid the Beltane fire,
And seal the Circle there.

May Song

Ring your garlands round the goat,
Make a maypole of his horns.
First to ring his shaggy throat
Has won the crown of thorns.

To the Devil be you wed,
Cunning maiden, Queen of May,
Soon to seek a satyr's bed
Amid the moss and hay.

Beltane

The wicker man is burning
Upon the verdant green.
The Witches' Wheel is turning,
We hail our Maytime Queen.

We crown ourselves with flowers,
And prance the maypole round,
Until the twilight hours,
While cries of death resound.

Triumphant flames of summer
Leap off the looming pyre;
A rabbit-maskèd mummer
Adores the raging fire.

The wicker man is burning,
We pay our yearly due.
The Witches' Wheel is turning,
From death comes life anew.

The Wicker Woman

A giant Goddess wrought of woven withe
Stands beautiful above the pagan green;
A nymph-like Priestess pays the yearly tithe—
The chosen consort of the Maytime Queen.

Condemned to die amid the wooden womb—
Yet having known pure rapture, perfect lust—
The Sacrifice accepts his flaming doom,
Knowing the corn will flourish from his dust.

The Wicker Woman, now with pregnant hips,
Takes him for child amid this Maytime rite,
While from the Priestess' wine-purpled lips
Echo the cries that marked their coupling's height.

Still bent across the altar, wine-cup spilt,
With flowers crowned, she meets the Green Man's gaze,
And with the dimmest sadness, ghost of guilt,
She sees her lover vanish in the blaze.

Witch Summons

Assume your sable robe,
O daughter of the dark!
The bats awake, and hark!—
Beneath the marble globe
Of Luna hoots the owl;
The toad from fenlands foul
Come flopping forth to mark
A daughter of the dark!

'Tis Sabbat Night, my lass!
So take your torch in hand,
And through the wooded land
With stealthy footstep pass.
The Coven now awaits,
O witch whose demon mates
Would join your saraband . . .
So take your torch in hand.

The Witch

There dwelt a witch within the wood,
The Devil's darksome land,
Who winked beneath a scarlet hood,
An apple in her hand.

Her glamour made her seem more fair
Than any mortal lass,
And none who found her forest lair
Returned from there, alas.

She led the children all astray
Into her mossy hut,
With promise of a game to play—
She never told them what.

The bodiced beauty soon bewitched
The boys with kisses red;
The girls with Satan soon were hitched;
And babes were ground for bread.

The Benighted Path

(Upon reading *The Benighted Path* by Richard Gavin)

The greenish glow of Algol hung
Above the woods, a poison lamp ·
To guide me as I delved among
The cypress trees and creeping damp.

A strange, benighted path I trod
Against the Gorgon's dreadful gaze,
But hardly frozen, overawed,
I reveled in her venomed rays.

I reveled in the goblin growths
Of mushrooms thrusting from the soil;
I spoke the old, nocturnal oaths,
At one with things that crawl and coil.

I sought the altars of the night
To pay my worship at them all.
By sable tapers' bluish light,
I knelt by tombs majestical.

I wore grotesque and withered masks
That hung from tangled willow boughs.
Mine was the most sublime of tasks—
The primal Monstrous Soul to rouse.

In pandaemonic ecstasy,
I sought the Night Mare's bone-wrought nest,
The Night Primeval pressing me
As I pursued the fleshless quest.

Ode to the Gorgon

Ode to the Gorgon

(Inspired by *The Benighted Path* by Richard Gavin)

O Goddess, O Gorgon whom Algol begems
As emerald malefic on grim diadems,
O tear off your tunic by seams and by hems—
Medusa! Medusa! deliver your dread!

O Goddess, O Gorgon with serpentine hair,
Who turns all my lust unto stone with your stare,
I willingly wander inside of your lair—
Medusa! Medusa! deliver your dread!

O Goddess, O Gorgon with parted red lips
And fangs whence the venom of nightmare oft drips,
From blood-founts of horror my spirit oft sips—
Medusa! Medusa! deliver your dread!

O Goddess, O Gorgon, Medusa by name,
O Lilith's own sister, O temptress untame,
O queen of dark Shakti ignite the black flame!—
Medusa! Medusa! deliver your dread!

O Goddess, O Gorgon, benighted I bow
Before your fair image and snake-woven brow!
O gaze on me, Gorgon, O gaze on me now!—
Medusa! Medusa! deliver your dread!

The Night Mare

(Inspired by *The Benighted Path* by Richard Gavin)

The Night Mare rides on darkling tides
Of shade and sacred horror,
And should you dare to mount the Mare,
You'll yearn forever for her.

Down winding ways, beneath the rays
Of Algol's ghoulish gleaming,
She'll charge full force; and grim's the course
Where ride the dead and dreaming.

The Hinterland at every hand
With nests of bone is littered;
She harvests them, each ivory gem,
From graves where they have glittered.

The Night Mare's tread leaves trails of dread
In wilds accurst and blighted,
The crescent moon her secret rune,
A boon to the benighted.

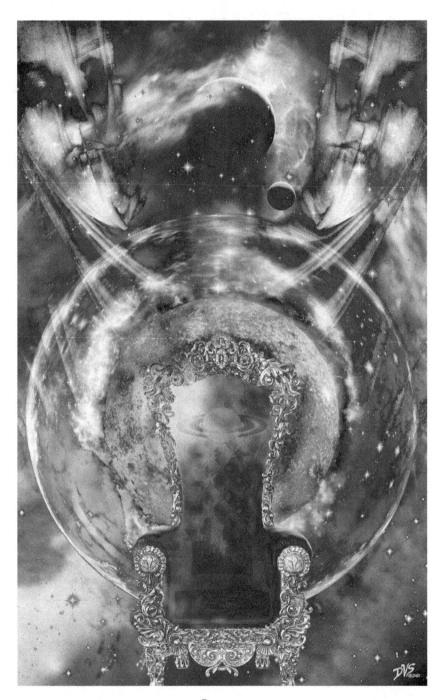

Saturna

Saturna

Insatiable Saturna, Queen of Night,
Voluptuous, with vast, benighted curves,
You drink the stream of Time, which downward swerves
In one great gyre of dying, greenish light.
Your thighs are girdled round with galaxies,
And you are crowned with nameless moons and stars,
But neither these, nor worlds we once called ours,
Can long avoid your yawning mysteries.

You suck the cosmos through your vampire lips,
And though the pull is imperceptible,
Your tide of doom is ineluctable,
And countless suns will drown in your eclipse.
You are the Black Hole, and beyond your kiss
There lies the final hell, the last abyss.

Nightshade Flowers

Your Mask of Porcelain

Your mask of porcelain,
Of pleasure or of pain,
Is like the visage of a ghost,
A moon that's on the wane.

Expressionless and pale
Beneath your silver veil,
It is your mask I love the most,
Your sad and silent tale.

Harlequin

Painted like a playing card,
Collared with a ruff of lace,
Long of lash and darkly starred
Are the eyes that haunt your face—
Silent eyes that sound my soul
From your pale and heart-shaped face.

Harlequin, a scarlet heart
Paints your pouting lips of white;
Mute was all your motley art,
Merely mimed our kiss that night—
Wordless kiss you coldly stole
At the masque one dreamful night.

Carnival Siren

The carnival has come to town
With music, games, and laughter;
When twilight falls, a pretty clown
Would have me follow after.

She beckons with a red balloon,
In lace-white ruff and corset;
Beneath a wicked, yellow moon,
She flirts—but does not force it.

It is my choice to heed her call,
My choice to take the ticket—
I chase the painted sideshow doll,
Cheered onward by a cricket.

It is my choice to turn the stile,
A lost and nameless number,
And roam the Midway, aisle on aisle,
Through realms of dream and slumber. . . .

The Ferris Wheel scowls above,
The Fun House grins so grimly;
The harlot waves with velvet glove,
Awaiting me so dimly.

The Hall of Mirrors claims my soul,
But none will know or miss me;
Her lipstick leaves a scarlet coal—
She strokes cold glass to kiss me.

Crimson Masquerade

A thousand rooms of crimson masquerade,
A thousand scenes of death, and secret lust.
In comic motley all are now arrayed—
A clumsy kiss of masks that turn to dust.
The harlequins, like garish marionettes,
Jerk helter-skelter in a ghastly dance;
This is the most fantastical of fêtes—
Yet this is but a morbid game of chance.

Chaos incarnate roams these gloomy halls,
A vast and formless demon many-legged;
Puppets of entropy, delusions dolls,
The masquers form a monster that has plagued
Humanity from since the dawn of time,
His every moment but a jester's rhyme.

Cassilda Dons the Pallid Mask

Cassilda, dear, I bid you now unclothe
From out your scarlet dress, and dance beneath
The ebon stars, your only robe and wreath
Black Hali's exhalations, which betroth
You unto me—your King! The Yellow King!
Put on the Pallid Mask, and dance, and sing.

Not upon me, O King, do place the Mask!
I am no queen to rule Carcosa, old
And dead with awful aeons lost, untold!—
Not upon me! My naked face would bask
In red Aldebaran's adoring beam!—
No!—I shall not!—Camilla!—I shall scream!

The Mask becomes you, fair Cassilda, nude,
Delirious mistress of the Hyades,
Whose dreadful dance will bring unto their knees
The sons of Man. A deadly lassitude
Dreams in your limbs, and what a monstrous song
Escapes your lips—it is not long, not long—!

Black Widow

The widow weaves her silver web
With silken words—deceptive, sweet.
The blood of life begins to ebb
As deadly venom takes its seat.

The crimson mark of harlots brands
Her sleek and sable abdomen.
Her graceful, slender-fingered hands
Play harp upon the fates of men.

Her figure is an hourglass
Whose doomful moments number few.
From out her bosom's warm crevasse
A spider clambers into view.

The widow waits within her lair
Amid the webbed remains of men
Who thought her deathly features fair,
And went the way of moth and wren.

Black Widow

Medusa

A hissing nest of sable serpents plays
Around her ivory neck, like living hair.
Her yellow eyes are beryls all ablaze
With ancient lust, and petrifying stare.

All who behold her beauty turn to stone,
And taste her poison passion all too late;
Her crimson kisses smother every moan
Of men that suffer petrifaction's fate.

Men came to kill a devil in a cave,
But were beguiled to find a Goddess there.
Her honeyed voice and sultry perfume drave
Them all to gaze upon her visage fair. . . .

Before those crumbling monuments of men,
Medusa flaunts her charms forevermore,
In melancholic dreams that once again
She is the gold-haired maiden loved of yore.

The Crimson Witch

For A. D.

Her mouth was like a crimson bloom,
With blood-red nectar, dark and rich.
I knew that I had met my doom
The night I kissed the crimson witch.
Amid the crimson-candled gloom,
No more than an enchanted lich,
I serve her from beyond the tomb,
For I have kissed the crimson witch.

Devil's Valentine

For A. D.

All dressed in red, with lips like burning blood,
You are a devil, O my valentine!
You sip a poison, satyr-trampled wine;
Your mere appearance sets my heart a-thud!

We trade our angels in for pitchforked imps,
Which prance around through scarlet candlelight.
The hearts we trade are goblin barbs—tonight
Of darkest passions we will share a glimpse. . . .

Daemonic Nathicana

I watched as divine Nathicana
Returned to the garden of Zaïs,
The zephyr-lulled garden of Zaïs,
Where lounges the lazy iguana.
I watched her descend to her dais,
Her pink-stoned and sphinx-holden dais,
Daemonic, encrimsoned with mana,
The queenly, the cold Nathicana.

She bore on her brow red Banapis,
A crescent like horns of a daemon,
A sinful and star-fallen daemon
With eyes like deep pools of black lapis.
I longed for my long-ago leman,
In yesteryear's labyrinth my leman,
A man who knows not where his map is,
Bewildered 'neath blood red Banapis.

She walked on the breath blown from Yabon,
Did ebony-tressed Nathicana,
The scarlet-mouthed whore Nathicana,
At autumn, the day men call Mabon.
And over the flora and fauna—
Marmoreal flora and fauna—
She shed ruby light that looked drab on
Fair Zaïs, 'neath Dzannin-cursed Yabon.

—After "Nathicana," by H. P. Lovecraft

The Laughter of Ghouls

Queen of Nenuphars

For A. D.

Nocturnal orchids, fallen stars
Fantastically flowering,
Compare not to the nenuphars
Your beauty is embowering.

Exotic as the orchid is,
I choose the blossom of your mouth—
Your scarlet tongue that forkèd is,
Whose nectar quenches all my drouth.

I choose the lilies in your eyes,
Which star your glamored gaze of blue—
The glint of candlelight that dies
As longingly I gaze on you.

But most of all, my queen, I choose
The nenuphar that shapes your soul;
I touch it, careful not to bruise
Its beauty, lest I pay the toll.

My Lady of the Nightshade Flower

For A. D.

My lady of the nightshade flower,
Your eyes of twilit dwale
Have gazed upon Endymion,
Who dreams in yonder vale.

My lady of the nightshade flower,
Your poison purple lips
Have whispered spells in blooming hells
Where honeyed nectar drips.

My lady of the nightshade flower,
Your sable, fragrant hair
Is crowned with wreaths whose blossom breathes
Dim drugs upon the air.

My lady of the nightshade flower,
Whose flesh is petal-pale,
O sing your songs, for evening longs
For belladonna's bale.

The Forest Witch

The witch that haunts the forest
Comes out at dusk of day,
When sunlight is the poorest,
And throws its last red ray.

Each night she takes a lover,
A handsome man will do.
While Venus burns above her,
She stirs her witch's brew.

Her Aphrodisian philter
Puts off a poison mist;
The forest falls off kilter,
The trees begin to list. . . .

A succubus, she's borne on
The drugged and slumbrous brume;
While Dian puts her horn on,
Endymion meets his doom.

A flash of flesh, a specter
Curvaceous, vampire-pale,
Her kiss imparts the nectar
Of aconite and dwale.

Her bosom full and stifling,
She suffocates her prey,
And sweetly laughs while trifling
With men soon thrown away.

The Blood Garden

The roses there are of a redder shade;
The scarlet orchids rear from crimson mist;
And she whom they have kissed
The naked flesh of walks there unafraid,
Oft lending her warm wrist. . . .

The flowers feast upon her offered flesh—
Vermillion lilies bite with tiny teeth,
And form a writhing wreath
Around her warm, white waist to taste the fresh
Hot blood that thuds beneath.

O ecstasy of mouths that feasting fall
Upon her neck, curved back in utter bliss!
She lies in an abyss
Of poison pleasure, moaning in the thrall
Of things that suck and hiss.

Her bosom burns beneath a bloody moon
Luridly leering through the sanguine haze;
Beneath its lustful gaze,
The ruddy ivy binds her limbs. . . . How soon
Her body, rapt, obeys.

The Demon of Ennui

I dreamed a monstrous slug crawled over me,
As I lay sprawled 'neath pale and rotting stars,
Which slid in sickly bars
Like cosmic slime down night's eternity.

It was as cold and clammy as the dead,
And suctioned onto me without remorse;
It filched my vital force
Like to a vampire dying to be fed.

Soon it transformed into a woman's shape,
Voluptuous, with lips like burning blood,
Her hair a drifting flood
Of crimson curls that promised no escape.

She smothered me with her voracious mouth,
And with her bosom's pallid amplitude—
Her beauty, though, imbued
With something like a shadow's waxing growth. . . .

How long I lay amid her strange embrace,
How long I dreamed that nightmare-tainted dream,
With muffled moan and scream,
I do not know—of time I lost all trace.

I only knew that she was slick with slime,
And that she somehow suctioned to my skin;

The Demon of Ennui

Unholy was our sin—
So blasphemous, and yet, somehow, sublime. . . .

The succubus grew listless after this,
Lying upon me with her awful weight,
And in my wretched state,
I could do naught but take her wicked kiss.

The sleepy demon mired me in her ooze,
Green ectoplasm soon engulfing me—
And still, eternally,
There clings an emerald murk I cannot lose.

The Mushroom Siren

Amid an autumn hollow,
A ring of fungus grew—
A crown of sickly yellow
Bediamonded with dew.

It rose so very slowly
From out the mulchy loam,
Until, awoken wholly,
A woman witched the gloam.

She was a mushroom woman,
With pale and tainted skin—
A siren almost human,
Who promised hyphal sin.

Through dark and silky tresses,
The fruiting fungus horned;
Her waist like dancers' dresses
A gill-frilled shelf adorned.

Her legs were joined together,
And rooted to the dirt;
She kept upon her tether,
Intelligent, alert.

Her gaze was white and filmy,
And in my heart took root.

I wondered—would it kill me
To taste this toadstool's fruit?

What psychotropic poison
Was in her mushroom flesh?—
I dreamed of our liaison
In mycorrhizal mesh. . . .

Her spores had surely planted
This madness in my mind—
But nonetheless, enchanted,
I left all light behind.

I drew so very near her,
And kissed her dark red lips.
The twilight woods grew drearer
With mushroom-cap eclipse. . . .

At last she dragged me under
The hungry, yielding clay,
Where, filled with dread and wonder,
I dream until this day.

The Fungal Nymph

She leaves a trail of toadstools where she walks,
And wears for crown a mushroom diadem;
And tiny toadstools from her lashes stem;
And there is something strange about her locks—
The way those living raven tresses twine
Around my flesh as with some fell design.

Although she has such lovely violet eyes,
Dark kykeon pours through her purple kiss;
And though her limbs' embrace is all my bliss,
They are not pale like other nymphs I prize—
They are a fungous gray, and half as warm,
Her slender fingers vaguely strange in form.

And yet her sweet, seductive whispers lull
Me into trance. . . . She pants forth perfumed spores,
Of which I deeply breathe through mouth and pores;
Her parasitic fingertips my skull
Invade with every loving, slow caress—
Just why they linger there I dare not guess.

Her amanita-mottled bosom bears
Me off to shadowed lands of mushroom-dreams,
As slumbering I lie there, fungal gleams
Of moonlight spurring what the sun impairs—
The thousand toadstools fruiting from my flesh,
Oblivious, as man and mushroom mesh.

The Fungal Nymph

Her Fungal Glance

Her milky eyes, her mushroom colored eyes,
Regard me strangely with a fungal glance.
From fanning lashes tiny toadstools rise,
Fluttering softly in a magic trance.

Her starlight tresses almost are too fine,
The errant strands adrift on breathless air.
Her pale lips open and our tongues entwine—
A twist of mushrooms we'll forever share.

The Fungal Fog

I never should have traveled to this place
Of sharp, black peaks that stab the starry sky;
I should have shunned this castle looming high
Like a black crown, with spires affronting space.

And yet the sapphire phare of Sirius
Allured me up the thousand ebon steps,
My spirit prey to spectral cordyceps—
A fungal fog with creepers perilous.

A withered king sat moldering within,
Upon an onyx throne, his flesh gone gray,
And from a mouth still moaning in dismay,
Poured forth the fog like some escaping sin.

Enwrapped in vapors, pulled as by a rope,
I soon approached the mummied monarch's throne,
To stand before that rotting king, alone,
Where stars proclaimed their fatal horoscope.

And then the corpse, a leprous puppet, rose,
To breathe the fungal fog adown my mouth—
Ere it collapsed to dust of lunar drouth,
A clanging crown to mark an empire's close.

Now I am king in this forsaken place,
Host of a fungus from a distant star.
I slowly waste, enslaved, the avatar
Of something come to humble man's proud race.

The Book of Black Dreams

A yawning gargoyle vaguely humanoid
Adorns the book worn black with centuries.
It screams the silence of the outer void,
And also whispers sphinx-like mysteries.
A sable serpent spills from out its lips,
And disappears across the dusty floor;
The brazen clasp that arabesquely grips
The monstrous text unlocks on restless lore. . . .

The pages open in a flapping storm,
Revealing yellowed velum blank as dreams—
Only a mushroomed warren of the worm
Remains amid the grimoire's rotting seams—
A growing hole of crumbling, black decay,
Wherein the world begins to fall away.

Black Oracles

For D. L. Myers

Tell us the darkest secrets from your soul—
Black oracles that bubble from the well
Where foetid toadstools, with their roots in hell,
Take on the forms of goblin, gnome, and troll.

Tell us the whispers from the space between
Primeval trees where darkness ever lurks—
Where hooded druids brave the moss-veiled murks
To hold their torch-lit rites on Halloween.

Reveal to us what venom evil flowers
Weep on the epitaphs of poets lost
To time and name, to melt the words embossed
Upon their tombs through slow, resistless hours.

Reveal to us the visions evermore
Nigh overflowing from your haunted heart,
And with the savage charging of the hart,
Lead us beyond the faerie-lighted tor.

Among the Gargoyles

I have seen what these gargoyles have gazed on
From their perilous perches of stone;
I have known what it is to grow crazed on
The mauve mist and the moonlight alone;
And high loneliness, too, I have known.

I have met the mad stare of Polaris
With white eyes just as cold and as hard;
On this ancient cathedral of Paris,
Most grotesque, I am ever its guard,
A mere ghoul irreversibly marred.

I have watched from the shadows as women
In white gowns have considered the ledge. . . .
I have felt heart and soul start to dimmen
As, averting my visage, I pledge
Not to startle them over the edge.

In my dreams to the moon I have traveled,
On such wings as don't waken by day—
But the vision is ever unraveled
By these gargoyles, these lords of dismay,
Whose gray wings are but anchors that stay.

Among the Gargoyles

Nocturnal Forest Cathedral

The evening sky above is veined with black;
High branches weave a bat-infested vault.
The old cathedral's somber, carved basalt
Is not more grand than this benighted track.

Mary of the Rosy Grave

Mary 'neath the weeping willow,
Mary of the rosy grave,
I would make for me a pillow
'Mid your bosom's ivory nave.

Mary in your ruby bedding,
Mary like a moon-white gem,
Soon shall be our blessèd wedding,
Mushroom-ring our diadem.

Mary, dead and yet undying,
Mary, uncorrupt of rot,
I have heard you softly sighing
In your warm and perfumed plot.

Mary, I have heard the demon;
Mary, does he tell me lies?
Mary, make of me your leman—
Mary, drink my soul and rise.

—After Adam Bolivar's "The Lay of Dumah"

Villanelle of My Dead Love

My love now slumbers in her grave,
As fair as any fallen star,
Beneath the flow of Lethe's wave.

If not within her velvet cave,
Her maiden charms embalmed here are—
My love now slumbers in her grave.

The ivory flesh the angels gave
To her, her eyes of icy spar . . .
Beneath the flow of Lethe's wave!

—Yet these and this my verse shall save:
Her mane of burning cinnabar.
My love now slumbers in her grave.

The scarlet mouth that hotly clave
To mine here flames, though she is far,
Beneath the flow of Lethe's wave.

Her bosom here is still my nave,
Though in her funeral simar,
My love now slumbers in her grave,
Beneath the flow of Lethe's wave.

The Voice of the Waves

There's a voice in the wind and the waves,
In the mist and the shimmering foam,
And I fear, yes I fear, when I hear it,
For I know I shall never come home.

For the siren who sings is the sea,
And I love her more dearly than death.
In the night has the nymph of her spirit
Blown my face with her icy cold breath.

There's a voice in the wind and the waves,
And I waken and walk by the shore
In the dark as the moon dreams above me,
And the stars are so cryptic and hoar.

For the siren who sings is the sea,
And I always have answered her call,
For she loves like no woman can love me,
And my soul is at home in the squall.

My Ship of Dreams

The silken sails are filled with wind,
And with the moon's blue beams,
And ere the silver mist has thinned,
I board my ship of dreams.

I sail across the seas unknown,
On slumber's aimless streams,
With stars and silence all alone,
Aboard my ship of dreams.

The sirens of enchanted isles,
With flesh that wetly gleams,
Allure me with resistless wiles,
And tempt my ship of dreams.

But I remain horizon-bound,
Indifferent to their schemes.
Fair lands with golden sunrise crowned
Await my ship of dreams.

I keep my lone and stalwart course,
Past shattered quinquiremes.
And yet I feel a dim remorse
Aboard my ship of dreams—

For I will nevermore return
To realms of men, it seems,
My one companion my own urn,
Aboard my ship of dreams.

Heart Burial

Bury my heart in a tomb, not my body,
Bury my heart in an urn all its own.
Bury my heart not in cerements cloddy,
Bury my heart as a relic in stone.

Carry my heart from my wormy cadaver,
Carry my heart to a safe, sacred place.
Carry my heart from the ghouls' evil slaver,
Carry my heart in a scarlet-trimmed case.

Bury my heart in a mournful old marker,
Bury my heart in the stories and tales.
Bury my heart on a day that is darker,
Bury my heart when the autumn wind wails.

Tarry, my heart, in your ivy-girt vessel,
Tarry, my heart, in your urn evermore.
Tarry, my heart, where the worms cannot nestle,
Tarry, my heart—though you love nevermore.

Requiem

The candles burn a somber blue
With deep lament
For me, the dead, with naught to do
But sleep here, pent
In scarlet cask whereon they threw
Their flowers, and went.

Funeral

A somber bell is ringing
This eve, and sad the sound
That sends the bats a-winging
Into the deep profound
Of purple forest clinging
To crimson-shrouded ground.

The tapers in the chapel
Where once I wed my bride
Burn blue; their shadows dapple
The nave where larvae glide.
With ghouls my corpse must grapple,
I who so young have died.

My coffin, strown with roses
Delivered by my love,
In holy gloom reposes—
None but her sable glove
Can be the one that closes
My cask to heaven above.

A somber bell is tolling
This eve, how sad to hear,
And graveyard fog is rolling
Across the woodland drear.
My love's fair head is lolling,
Begemmed by many a tear.

Acknowledgments

"Absinthia," *Spectral Realms* No. 4 (February 1, 2016).

"Among the Gargoyles," *Spectral Realms* No. 4 (February 1, 2016).

"Among the Ghouls," *Spectral Realms* No. 2 (January 31, 2015).

"Beltane," *Weirdbook* No. 41 (November 2018).

"The Benighted Path," *Ravenwood Quarterly* No. 2 (Fall 2016).

"The Black Czarina," *Necronomicum: The Magazine of Weird Erotica* No. 3 (July 17, 2015).

"Black Oracles," *Oracles from the Black Pool* by D. L. Myers (Hippocampus Press, October 2019).

"Blood and Beauty," *Weird Fiction Review* No. 6 (July 1, 2016).

"The Blood Garden," *Spectral Realms* No. 2 (Winter 2015).

"Carmilla," *Skelos* No. 2 (March 1, 2017).

"Carnival Siren," *Caravans Awry* (Planet X Publications, October 2018).

"Cassilda Dons the Pallid Mask," *Cyäegha* No. 16 (Summer 2016).

"Clarethea," *Spectral Realms* No. 3 (August 1, 2015).

"The Crimson Witch," *Eye to the Telescope* No. 30 (October 2018).

"Daemonic Nathicana," *Weirdbook Annual* No. 2 (Winter 2018).

"The Demon of Ennui," *The Audient Void* No. 8 (October 2019).

"Eventide," *Darkling's Beasts and Brews: Poetry with a Drink on the Side* (Lycan Valley Publications, Winter 2018).

"Flame-Mistress of the Morning Star," *Eternal Haunted Summer* (Summer 2019).

"Funeral," *The Audient Void* No. 3 (Spring 2017).

"The Fungal Nymph," *Necronomicum: The Magazine of Weird Erotica* No. 2 (February 11, 2015).

"The Ghost Carriage," *Weirdbook* No. 33 (October 27, 2016).

"A Ghostly Lily," *The Phantasmagorical Promenade* (Planet X Publications, Spring 2019).

"Harlequin," *Floppy Shoes Apocalypse 3* (Nocturnicorn Books 2017).

"The Harpy," *The Audient Void* No. 1 (June 19, 2016).

"Her Ghostly Sigh," *Weird Fiction Review* No. 7 (Winter 2016).

"In Fits of Wildest Dreaming," *Spectral Realms* No. 3 (August 1, 2015).

"In the Dead of Winter," *Winter Horror Days* (Omnium Gatherum Media, December 2015).

"Invocation of Diana," *Eternal Haunted Summer* (Summer 2016).

"Krampus," *Feverish Fiction* No. 1 (December 2016).

"The Lady in Scarlet," *Weirdbook* No. 33 (October 27, 2016).

"The Lady in White," *HWA Poetry Showcase* No. 3 (August 7, 2016).

"The Lady of the Graves," *Gothic Blue Book* No. 5 (October 28, 2015).

"The Laughter of Ghouls," *Weirdbook* No. 31 (September 14, 2015).

"Lilith," *Eternal Haunted Summer* (Summer 2017).

"Lucia," *Weird Fiction Review* No. 8 (Winter 2017).

"Mary of the Rosy Grave," *Spectral Realms* No. 7 (Fall 2017).

"Medusa," *The Audient Void* No. 1 (June 19, 2016).

"Midnight in the Ebon Rose Bower," *Skelos* No. 1 (May 26, 2016).

"The Mushroom Siren," *The Audient Void* No. 4 (Fall 2017).

"My Lady of the Nightshade Flower," *Diary of a Sorceress* by Ashley Dioses (Hippocampus Press, October 2017).

"Ode to Ashtoreth," *Weirdbook* No. 32 (June 16, 2016).

"Ode to the Gorgon," *Eternal Haunted Summer* (Summer 2018).

"Portrait of the Countess," *Weird Fiction Review* No. 6 (July 1, 2016).

"A Queen of Carpathia," *Weirdbook* No. 35 (May 20, 2017).

"Queen of the Bats," *Weirdbook* No. 35 (May 20, 2017).

"The Shadow of the Reaper," *Gothic Blue Book* No. 5 (October 28, 2015).

"To Court the Night," *Black Wings VI: New Tales of Lovecraftian Horror*, ed. S. T. Joshi (PS Publishing, 2017).

"Transylvanian Darkness," *Spectral Realms* No. 5 (Summer 2016).

"The Vampire-Slayer's Whip," *Devil's Armory* (Horrified Press 2015).

"Walpurgis Eve," *Weirdbook* No. 31 (September 14, 2015).

"Werewolf," *Spectral Realms* No. 4 (February 1, 2016).

"When Wolfsbane Blooms," *Weirdbook* No. 35 (May 20, 2017).

"The Woman in the Feathered Mask," *Skelos* No. 3 (Summer 2017).

"Woodland Funeral," *Weirdbook* No. 33 (October 27, 2016).

"Your Mask of Porcelain," *Feverish Chixxx* No. 3 (Winter 2017).